OXFORD
UNIVERSITY PRESS

Great Clarendon Street, Oxford, OX2 6DP,
United Kingdom

Oxford University Press is a department of the
University of Oxford. It furthers the University's
objective of excellence in research, scholarship,
and education by publishing worldwide. Oxford is a
registered trade mark of Oxford University Press in the
UK and in certain other countries

Text © Oxford University Press 2023

The moral rights of the author have been asserted

First Edition published in 2023

All rights reserved. No part of this publication may
be reproduced, stored in a retrieval system, or
transmitted, in any form or by any means, without the
prior permission in writing of Oxford University Press,
or as expressly permitted by law, by licence or under
terms agreed with the appropriate reprographics
rights organization. Enquiries concerning
reproduction outside the scope of the above should
be sent to the Rights Department, Oxford University
Press, at the address above.

You must not circulate this work in any other form and
you must impose this same condition on any acquirer

British Library Cataloguing in Publication Data

Data available

ISBN: 978-1-382-04342-7

10 9 8 7 6 5 4 3 2

The manufacturing process conforms to the
environmental regulations of the country of origin.

Printed in China by Golden Cup

Acknowledgements

Chander and the Chimps written by Paul Shipton;
Animals on the Map written by Anita Ganeri

Illustrated by Pauline Gregory and Kate McLelland

Author photos courtesy of Vicky Shipton and
Anita Ganeri

The publisher and authors would like to thank the
following for permission to use photographs and
other copyright material:

Cover: Iyeyee / Shutterstock; antpkr / Shutterstock.
Maps: p31, 33, 35, 37, 39, 41, 43: Sylvain SONNET
/ 123RF. Photos: p29(t): TippaPatt / Shutterstock;
p29(b): AB Photographie / Shutterstock; p30(t):
Gunter Nuyts / Shutterstock; p30(b): Jose A. Bernat
Bacete / Moment / Getty Images; p31(t): Nature
Picture Library / Alamy Stock Photo; p31(b): Cyril
Ruoso / Minden Pictures / Getty Images; p32-33:
Shane Gross / Shutterstock; p33(tl): GAO5555 /
Shutterstock; p33(tr): Pally / Alamy Stock Photo;
p33(m): wildestanimal / Getty Images; p33(bl):
Nicolas-SB / Shutterstock; p33(br): Matt9122 /
Shutterstock; p34: apple2499 / Shutterstock; p35:
AB Photographie / Shutterstock; p36(t): Quayside
/ Shutterstock; p36(b): Juniors Bildarchiv GmbH
/ Alamy Stock Photo; p37(tt): Mirror-Images
/ Shutterstock; p37(tb): antpkr / Shutterstock;
p37(b1): Abhindia / Shutterstock; p37(b2): Ukki
Studio / Shutterstock; p37(b3): cowboy54
/ Shutterstock; p37(b4): Erni / Shutterstock; p37(b5):
Eugene Troskie / Shutterstock; p37(b6): Miriam
Newitt / Shutterstock; p38(t): valex61 / Shutterstock;
p38(b): Patife / Shutterstock; p39(t): yakub88
/ Shutterstock; p39(ml): Vera NewSib / Shutterstock;
p39(mr): Sahad mt / Shutterstock; p39(bl): Andrey_
Kuzmin / Shutterstock; p39(bm): Pakhnyushchy
/ Shutterstock; p39(br): awol666 / Shutterstock; p40:
aleksander hunta / Shutterstock; p41: gorkhe1980
/ Shutterstock; p42: TippaPatt / Shutterstock; p43(t):
Maria Sivtseva / Shutterstock.

Every effort has been made to contact copyright
holders of material reproduced in this book. Any
omissions will be rectified in subsequent printings if
notice is given to the publisher.

In this book ...

Chander and the Chimps 7

Animals on the Map......................27

Have a go!

pond

tusk

chest

paint

In this book, we go deep into the forest. We will meet chimps!

Have you ever seen a chimp or a gorilla?

Chander and the Chimps

Written by Paul Shipton
Illustrated by Pauline Gregory

Chander was in his jeep.

"I am off to film the **CHIMPANZEES!**" he said.

When the jeep hit a bump, Chander's bag fell. It landed in the road. Chander **did not see** it.

He went to get his bag.

"My chair was in that bag ..." said Chander. "So was my lunchbox!"

It was a **tall** chimp ...
with Chander's **chair!**
A *shorter* chimp followed.
He had Chander's
lunchbox.

It was not much fun for Chander.

At last the **tall** chimp held up her hand. The fun ended.

She put the camera down near Chander. Then all the chimps RAN OFF.

"She must have felt sad for me," said Chander.

The camera's red light was on.

"I DID film the chimpanzees!" Chander said.

"This film is the **BEST!**"

Look back

In this book, we will meet bright parrots and hidden panthers.

STOP AND THINK

What might you see on a map?

Animals on the Map

Written by Anita Ganeri
Illustrated by Pauline Gregory

Contents

Chimpanzees 30
Sharks 32
Panthers 34
Frogs and toads 36
Parrots 38
Yaks 40
Bees 42
Look it up 44

>

We will follow the animals ...

in the sunlight

and at night.

Chimpanzees

Go deep into the **rainforest** to see chimpanzees.

They can lift BIG logs.

They are clever.

On the map

They can sleep in nests up high.

Sharks

Sharks are fast.

Sharks hunt fish and grab them with **SHARP** teeth.

We can see different sharks.

zebra

goblin

On the map

cat

Galapagos

lemon

Panthers

Panthers hunt for food at night in the forest.

Animals can not see the panther's dark fur.

On the map

Frogs and toads

You can tell them apart.

Frogs have **moist** skin.

Toads have bumps.

Frogs have long back legs for jumping.

Toads have short back legs.

On the map

Parrots

Parrots chatter in the forest.

A parrot picks up a nut with its foot.

It taps the nutshell with its **SHARP** bill to get in.

nutshell   bill

On the map

Yaks

Yaks have **thick** coats. The coats protect them in the *freezing wind*.

Yaks are up in the hills.

On the map

Bees

Look for bees in parks and gardens. Bees buzz as they collect **pollen**.

BUZZ

pollen

Bees have yellow and black bands. This tells animals to **AVOID** them.

On the map

Look it up

habitats: the spots animals are in

moist: a bit wet

pollen: a yellow powder that helps to form seeds

rainforest: a big forest that is hot and gets lots of rain

Ha! Ha!

How do bees get to the shops?

On the buzz!